NO PUN INTENDED

VOLUME TOO

BY

WILL LIVINGSTON

Other Books by Will Livingston

No Pun Intended

No Pun Intended: Volume Too
Second Edition Changes

Author's note added

On page 26, three original jokes
replaced with four canonical additions:

1. A joke from the original game was justifiably removed from *The Last of Us Part I* — and omitted from the first edition of this book — because it made light of dwarfism. A simple change makes it non-disparaging, and the revised version has been added.

2. The complete version of an interrupted joke told by Riley in season 1, episode 7 of HBO's *The Last of Us*.

3. A joke told by Joel to Ellie in *The Last of Us Part II*.

4. An adaptation of a joke told by Dina to Ellie in *The Last of Us Part II*.

This is a functional art piece created as an adaptation of a fictitious book that was first digitally represented in the acclaimed 2013 video game *The Last of Us*, which was written by Neil Druckmann, developed by Naughty Dog, and published by Sony Computer Entertainment

The title of this art piece, in its entirety, is:

NO PUN INTENDED
VOLUME TOO
by Will Livingston

BASED UPON ORIGINAL CONCEPTS WRITTEN BY
Neil Druckmann

AND COVER ART CREATED BY
Alexandria Neonakis

ADAPTED FOR TACTILE REALITY BY
Obie Williams / InkTree Creations

NEIL DRUCKMANN

is an Israeli-American writer, creative director, designer, and programmer who has been co-president of the video game developer Naughty Dog since 2020.
He can be followed on:
Twitter (@Neil_Druckmann)
Instagram (@Druckmann)

ALEXANDRIA NEONAKIS

is a freelance concept artist, fine artist, and illustrator from Nova Scotia Canada, currently residing in Los Angeles. Previously she was a senior concept artist at Wonderstorm and a character concept artist at Naughty Dog. Through her agents at Bright, she's worked with several publishers such as Simon & Schuster, Random House, Macmillan, Scholastic, and Inhabit Media.
Her work can be seen at:
alexneonakis.com
She can be followed on:
Twitter (@Beavs)
Instagram (@alexneonakis)

OBIE WILLIAMS

is an artist and author with big ideas and abysmal sleep habits. His fungus-free post-apocalyptic fantasy novel, *The Crimes of Orphans*, is available on Amazon.
His artwork can be seen at:
inktree.art
He can be followed on:
Twitter (@inktree_art)
Instagram (@inktree.art)

AUTHOR'S NOTE

The first twelve pages of jokes in each book of InkTree's
The Last of Us Joke Books series is identical. This is
intentional, as those pages contain the collected jokes that
are read in *The Last of Us* video game, the HBO adapted
series, and/or the *Left Behind* DLC. I felt it was only right
to give collectors access to all of the original jokes without
having to buy more than one book, and to give cosplayers
access regardless of which book they might pull out while
cosplaying.

After those twelve pages, all 400+ remaining jokes are
unique to their respective books. I have taken great pains
to be sure of this, even going to far as to use plagiarism-
detecting software against myself.

A small handful of jokes may use similar wordplay, but
those are few and far between, and no jokes should be
repeated verbatim between books (or, worse, in a single
book). If you, dear reader, happen to spot a mistake in this
regard, please email me at obie@obiewilliams.com.
I will immediately adjust my manuscript for further
printings, and send you a free copy of any one of my
books as a thank-you for your keen eye.

FOREWORD

This is for anyone, but most especially for Neil and Alexandria. It's the story of how *The Last of Us* first helped save my life, and then helped save my family's home. It's an explanation of why I felt compelled to make this, but also why I struggled with whether it was the right thing to do. But mostly, it's my apology in lieu of permission.

It began with a proton pack.

At the age of 6, I was obsessed with the Ghostbusters and, naturally, begged my mother for a proton pack to play with. Luckily, Mom was a big geek like I grew up to be, and she had a knack for crafts and sewing. She also worked in a hospital, from which she was able to procure a number of interesting supplies for crafting. So, from a pile of spare medical parts and her imagination, my mother made me a truly awesome proton pack, and I loved it dearly. Over thirty years later, the vague image of it in my head probably looks nothing like it really did, and what it did look like probably wasn't much like the packs in the movies . . . but I can vividly recall *feeling* like it was as real as the real thing, like I had my very own piece of a beloved story. And, like a good drug, it left me chasing that feeling ever since, trying to capture the euphoria through countless artistic pursuits of my own.

Fast forward to 2018: the worst year of my life I have ever experienced. I'll spare you the details, but suffice to say I found myself in a situation where my mental health was exceedingly poor and I was alone nearly all the time. In a desperate effort to prevent losing myself to unhealthy coping mechanisms, I started filling my time with two pursuits I enjoyed as a child, but had often neglected since becoming an adult: playing video games and making art for art's sake. The former began when a family member gave me a used PS4 and, upon searching for something to play, I stumbled upon a copy of *The Last of Us Remastered* for $5 at GameStop. As I walked out of the store with that game in hand, I had no way of knowing that it would end up being not only the first video game to ever make me cry (twice, in fact), but also that, in doing so, it would be the first thing to put a crack in the emotional walls I had built up to protect myself from the hardships I was dealing with.

My first journey in Joel and Ellie's world allowed me — for the first time in months — to find some respite from hourly thoughts of ending my life. As I made my way through that incredible story of love, loss, and enduring humanity in the face of untold horror, I found myself coming upon clear patches in a previously ubiquitous fog of my own loneliness and despair. By the end of the game, I still had a long road towards better health, but I finally felt like I had at least found a path to follow. Before that, I had . . . well, I had been lost in the darkness. *The Last of Us* was my light.

When I wasn't playing, I filled the rest of my alone time by working on my digital art skills — a passion I'd had since high school, but had been neglecting for a while. It was also during that time that, having been a Stephen King fan most of my life, I had put "see the release of *IT: Chapter Two*" in theaters" on my "reasons not to die" list (sometimes the short-term, small goals feel more achievable). Thus, I found myself admiring a lot of artwork relating to that story, but I noticed that everything seemed to incorporate Pennywise the Clown or red balloons. I wanted to see something that looked like it *really* came from that world, and that wouldn't showcase those things. From that notion came my first "in-universe" postcard design depicting the fictional town of Derry, Maine.

Fast-forward again to September, 2022. Three years had passed since I lived to see *IT: Chapter Two*. My Etsy store, InkTree Creations, had evolved from an avenue by which to share my earliest postcard designs to a full-time attempt at being a successful (i.e., pay the bills) artist. I had just finished a couple of hours being enraptured by the beauty of *The Last of Us Part I*, and I suddenly found myself wishing to own my very own personalized Firefly pendant. Etsy seemed like a natural go-to; I like supporting other artists. But while there were a couple of offerings that were clearly made with love by their respective creators, none quite fit my image of what I wanted for myself. I wanted something I could wear that looked and felt like it had been pulled straight from the game. Something that made me believe, for a moment, that I had really stepped foot in that world. Something that made me feel like a six-year-old with his very own proton pack.

So I went about making my own. And when I found that I was pleased with how it turned out, I decided — as I had with my postcards — that others might enjoy my labor of love. So I put my pendants on Etsy and, for the second time, had no way of knowing how much the world of *The Last of Us* was going to change my life for the better.

Not long after I debuted my pendants in early October, 2022, producing them became my full-time job, and InkTree had suddenly become pay-the-bills successful in all the ways I'd spent two years striving for it to be. And, just as when I had first discovered the game, the timing could not have been more crucial. That same month, my wife and I signed a one-year lease on a new home. Just eight weeks later — and less than three weeks before

Christmas — my previously-consistent supplemental contract work abruptly dried up *and* my wife's employer decided, out of the blue, to let her go. Suddenly, my wife, my child, and I were faced with uncertainty about the future of keeping the very roof over our heads. But once more, the world of *The Last of Us* saved me . . . saved *us* this time. Positive reviews of my pendants had started coming in and excitement over the debut of the HBO series was heating up, so in the moment we needed it most, the pendants suddenly became enough to help keep us in our home, allow us to have a happy holiday season, and take just enough time to breathe and figure out our next step away from the precipice of financial ruin.

Needless to say, our little family has been tuning in to watch the brilliant series every Sunday night. So when we saw a prop version of *No Pun Intended: Volume Too*, I wondered if any artist had tackled the task of creating a real-world adaptation. Not just a copy of the cover art surrounding a blank journal or 12 pages of just the jokes spoken in-game — but a legitimate attempt to make a fully-realized book of puns. Of course, nobody had, and so I started thinking about being the one to do it.

But I had some reservations. While many of my artistic offerings are based on popular works of fiction, they are all also equally original creations of my own. Furthermore, I hold myself to strict rules against lifting content from source materials. My postcards — an inherently photography-based medium — are only ever made from photographs or digital models which either: are created by me, reside within the public domain, or are shared under a Creative Commons CC0 or CC-BY license. My pendants, though they do incorporate the relatively simple geometric Firefly logo, also utilize a unique font of my own design, Cordyceps Sans, as well as a number of original techniques throughout their physical creation.

However, creating this book would be different. The cover art, specifically, was my biggest moral quandary. No matter what, it was going to have to be directly based on the original art seen in-game. The title, the fictional author name, and about four-dozen fairly generic puns . . . those I was more or less comfortable with reproducing, provided I expanded on the overall concept. But if I was going to feel comfortable recreating that cover art, I knew I was going to have to put my own work in, and actually *recreate* it, in the "ground-up" sense.

Over the course of a few weeks, I spent approximately 80 hours trying to do this right. I pored over countless screenshots of the book from every angle possible, in all its appearances throughout every game. I labored most heavily over recreating the blurb-inclusive back cover, which is rarely seen (it wasn't even reproduced on the show's prop). I clicked through game and TV show scenes frame-by-frame, taking notes on interior font use, formatting, jokes per page, even margin sizes. I compared spine thicknesses and height/width ratios to dozens of books on my own shelves, trying to sort out an estimated page count and trim size. Then, I went about curating roughly 400 additional puns to fit the page count I settled on.

Perhaps most daunting of all was spending an entire day trying to figure out who created the original cover image. I sifted through the portfolios of dozens of artists credited on the original game and came up with nothing. It was only through sheer luck of thinking up just the right Google keywords that I stumbled upon a nearly-decade-old Tumblr post by Alexandria Neonakis, in which she humbly shared her designs for all three of Ellie's joke books as almost an afterthought.

From there, I was able to examine her artwork created around the same time, and that helped me estimate what parts of her original design were meant to show the ravages of time, and what parts were supposed to have been original to the book. Was the fading at the corner of that triangle part of the cover design, or did the book lay partially exposed to sunlight for a while? Are those darker purple splotches meant to be water damage, or an Eric Carle-esque paint texture? Were all those words hand-lettered, or did they start as a font and were then altered for letter uniqueness? And *for the love of God, what does that barcode say?!*

This is getting long-winded, and you might be asking yourself, "Do I need to know any of this before I enjoy the puns?" To which I will answer with a quote from Morgan Freeman's Lucius Fox in *Batman Begins*: "Not at all. I just wanted you to know how hard it was."

The point is, as my late father was fond of saying: a job worth doing is worth doing right. My goal was to make a joke book as close as possible to what Ellie had in her world. To give any TLOU fan holding this a fraction of the joy felt by a little boy with a proton pack over thirty years ago. To pay forward some of the light that this franchise has given me in some of my darkest times. To anyone reading this, I hope you love it as much as I loved making it.

To Neil and Alexandria, I hope you will forgive me for not asking permission first. I think mostly I was afraid of chickening out, or of losing the creative fire that drove me forward on this project. If either of you want me to stop offering this, no official C&D is necessary. Just email me: obie@obiewilliams.com. I will completely understand. If it helps, I will be donating 25% of proceeds from sales of this item to the Girls Make Games Scholarship Fund. The rest will help my family continue to reclaim economic stability, and allow me to continue sharing art with the world.

– Obie

What did the triangle say to the circle?

You're so pointless.

What did the cannibal get when he showed up to the party late?

A cold shoulder!

I heard two peanuts walked into a park...

One was as-salted.

A boiled egg in the morning is really hard to beat.

I'm reading a book about

anti-gravity.

It's impossible to put down.

It's not that the guy didn't

know how to juggle...

He just didn't have the balls to do it.

I'm glad I know

sign language.

It's become quite handy.

I forgot how to throw a boomerang.

But it came back to me.

When a clock is hungry...

It goes back four seconds.

**I once heard a joke
about amnesia...**

But I forget how it goes.

**When the power went out
at the school...**

The children were de-lighted.

Those fish were shy.

They were obviously coy.

Those two men drinking battery acid

will soon be charged.

What is a pirate's

favorite letter?

'Tis the C.

I'm inclined...

To be laid back.

Newspaper headline reads:

Cartoonist found dead at home,

Details are sketchy.

The magician got frustrated

And pulled his hare out.

What did the frustrated cannibal do?

He threw up his hands.

A criminal's best asset...

Is his lie-ability.

I didn't have the faintest idea...

As to why I passed out.

I heard about the guy who got hit in the head with a can of soda.

He is lucky it was a soft drink.

There was once a crossed-eyed teacher...

Who had issues controlling his pupils.

Diarrhea is hereditary...

It runs in your genes.

How does a computer get drunk?

It takes screen shots.

It doesn't matter how much you push the envelope.

It'll still be stationary.

What did the Confederate soldiers use to eat off of?

Civil ware.

What did they use to drink with?

Cups. Dixie cups.

I walked into my sister's room and tripped on a bra.

It was a booby-trap.

A book just fell on my head.

I only have my shelf to blame.

**What is the leading cause of divorce in
long-term marriages?**

A stalemate.

**Bakers trade bread recipes on a
knead-to-know basis.**

**A moon rock tastes better than
an earthly rock...**

Because it's meteor.

**A backwards poet
writes in verse.**

I used to be addicted to soap.
But I'm clean now.

3.14% of sailors are pi rates.

**I stayed up all night wondering
where the sun went.**
Then it dawned on me.

**What did the mermaid
wear to her math class?**
An algae bra

Why did the scarecrow get an award?

Because he was outstanding in his field.

I tried to catch some fog earlier.

I mist.

You know what's not right?

Left.

**What does a pirate say
while eating sushi?**

Ahoy! Pass me some soy!

People are making apocalypse jokes like there's no tomorrow.

You wanna hear a joke about pizza?

Never mind, it was too cheesy.

If a dish towel could tell a joke, I think it would have a dry sense of humor

What did the green grape say to the purple grape?

Breathe, you idiot!

Will Livingston

Why can't a nose be 12 inches?

Because then it would be a foot.

The petite psychic escaped prison.

He was a small medium at large.

What do you call an alligator in a vest?

An investigator.

What is the downside to eating a clock?

It's time consuming.

**How could the woman tell that
her mare was getting sick?**

She sounded a little hoarse.

I went to a seafood disco last week...

And pulled a mussel.

Do you know where you can get chicken broth in bulk?

The stock market.

I cut my finger shredding cheese...

But I have grater problems.

My cat was just sick on the carpet.

I don't think it's feline well.

Will Livingston

**Why did the octopus
beat the shark in a fight?**
Because it was well-armed.

**Atheism is a
non-prophet organization.**

There's a new type of broom out.
It's sweeping the nation.

**What did the buffalo say when
he dropped his little boy off at school?**
Bison.

How was Rome split in two?
With a pair of Caesars.

The shovel was a
ground breaking invention.

Did you hear about the guy
who lost the left side of his body?
He's alright now.

What do you call a girl with
one leg that's shorter than the other?
Ilene.

I did a theatrical performance on puns.

It was a play on words.

What do you do with a dead chemist?

You barium.

I bet the person who created

the door knocker

Won a no-bell prize.

Thanks for explaining

the word "many" to me

It means a lot.

What do you call a beautiful pumpkin?
Gourdgeous.

What did the alien say
to the pitcher of water?
Take me to your liter.

What do you call a cow with no legs?
Ground beef.

What do you call a cow with two legs?
Lean beef.

Will Livingston

I used to be afraid of hurdles.

But I got over it.

What should you do if you are cold?

Stand in the corner.

It's 90 degrees.

How did the picture end up in jail?

It was framed!

Why did one banana

spy on the other?

Because she was appealing.

I heard about a soldier who survived mustard gas <u>and</u> pepper spray.

He was a seasoned veteran.

Why shouldn't you trust atoms?

They make up everything.

What's it called when you have too many aliens?

Extraterrestrials.

What do cows tell each other at bedtime?

Dairy tales.

Why didn't the lion win the race?

Because his opponent was a cheetah.

**What happens to nitrogen
when the sun comes up?**

It becomes daytrogen.

**What's it called when
you put a cow in an elevator?**

Raising the steaks.

Why did the tomato turn red?

Because it saw the salad dressing.

What do you call a line of rabbits marching backwards?

A receding hairline.

How do trees access the internet?

They log on.

Why should you never trust a train?

They have loco motives.

I saw an ad for burial plots and thought to myself...

This is the last thing I need.

I just found out I'm colorblind.

The diagnosis came completely out of the purple.

I'd tell you a chemistry joke...

But I know I wouldn't get a reaction.

I wondered why the baseball was getting bigger.

Then it hit me.

The wedding was so emotional...

Even the cake was in tiers.

What does a house wear?
A dress.

I owe a lot to the sidewalks.
They've been keeping me
off the streets for years.

Imagine if alarm clocks
hit you back in the morning.
It would be truly alarming.

Why is a skeleton a bad liar?
You can see right through it.

Will Livingston

I was accused of being a plagiarist.
Their words, not mine.

**A man sued an airline company
after they misplaced his luggage.**
Sadly, he lost his case.

Why do trees have so many talents?
They branch out.

**At my boxing club there is
only one punching bag.**
I hate waiting for the punch line!

An untalented gymnast...

Walked into a bar.

Einstein developed
a theory about space.

It was about time, too.

What do you get when you
ask a lemon for help?

Lemonaid.

Traveling on a flying carpet...

Is a rugged experience.

Will Livingston

The old woman who lived in a shoe wasn't the sole owner...

There were strings attached.

Did you hear about the crime in the parking garage?

It was wrong on so many levels.

Why are there fences on graveyards?

Because people are dying to get in.

Never trust an acupuncturist.

They'll stab you in the back.

**Models of dragons
are not to scale.**

**Never ask a mathematician
to explain infinity.**
It goes on forever.

**I know a couple who stopped
going to the gym.**
Their relationship didn't work out.

Debt collectors keep calling me.
They won't leave me a loan!

Will Livingston

People say I look better without glasses…

But I just can't see it.

**Don't judge a meal by
the look of the first course.**

It's very souperficial.

**What do you call
a young musician?**

A minor.

I broke my finger today.

On the other hand, I'm completely fine.

**I hear the postal service
is a mail-dominated industry.**

**Why isn't sun tanning
an Olympic sport?**

The best you can ever get is bronze.

What do you mean June is over?

Julying!

**Did you hear that the candle
quit his job?**

I guess he felt burnt out.

Will Livingston

I saw a magic tractor

on the road once.

It turned into a field!

I met some aliens from outer space.

They were pretty down to earth.

Who can remember a single

roman numeral?

I, for one.

How do mountains see?

They peak.

I told my friend she drew her eyebrows too high.

She seemed surprised.

The earth's rotation really makes my day.

If I buy a bigger bed will I have more or less bedroom?

A rope went running around a rough block.

Before long, it got a-frayed.

What kind of shoes do ninjas wear?

Sneakers.

What did the sea monster say after devouring a ship?

I can't believe I ate the hull thing.

Only small babies are delivered by stork.

Heavy ones need a crane.

My friend couldn't get over his breakup with a bartender.

He kept asking her for another shot.

I had a pun about insanity…
But then I lost it.

Why don't cannibals eat clowns?
Because they taste funny.

**Why did the Italian restaurant
have to close?**
Because it only made pennes.

**I thought I saw a spider
on my computer screen.**
Turns out it was just a bug.

Will Livingston

A doctor broke his arm
while auditioning for a play.
He made the cast though.

Ever heard the story of
the haunted refrigerator?
It's chilling.

Why are frogs so happy?
They eat whatever bugs them.

If you wear cowboy clothes
are you ranch dressing?

I was addicted to the hokey pokey.
But I turned myself around.

**I tried to carve a flute out of
a tree branch...**
But it wooden whistle.

Why didn't the bomb explode?
It refused.

**I bet mummies wouldn't be so stiff
if they saw a Cairo-practor.**

Will Livingston

I feel sorry for shopping carts.
They're always getting pushed around.

I went to a still life art show.
It was not moving at all.

When Halloween ends...
It's Octover.

**How do you make swine
groan instead of oink?**
Put them in a pig pun.
They find it boaring.

Why couldn't the dead car
drive into the cluttered garage?
Lack of vroom.

I like padlocks with dials because
they're easy to use and don't need a key.
It's a spinning combination.

What do superheroes like in their
drinks?
Just ice.

How does a penguin build its house?
Igloos it together

Time flies like an arrow.

Fruit flies like a banana.

How do you help hurt balloons?

Helium.

What did the hat say to the jacket?

"You go around back; I'll go on ahead."

How many tickles does it take

to make an octopus laugh?

Ten.

Ten tickles.

Why was the farmer a good drummer?

He knew how to keep a beet.

A man once asked if I had any German puns.

I told him, "Nein."

Did you hear about the invention of the white board?

It was remarkable.

Can February march?

No, but April may.

Matryoshka dolls are cute and all…

But they're just so full of themselves.

What do you do to an open wardrobe?

You closet.

**Why did Cold Hands Magazine
go out of business?**

Low circulation.

**Some aquatic mammals
escaped the zoo.**

It was otter chaos.

I have a complicated relationship with elevators.
Sometimes they're uplifting; other times they let me down.

My friend, Nick, couldn't loan me five cents.
He was Nicholas.

Where do you imprison a skeleton?
In a rib cage.

There's a fine line between a numerator and a denominator.

Will Livingston

I tried to be a barber...

But I wasn't cut out for it.

How did the microwave
fall in love with a piece of metal?

It got turned on, and sparks flew.

When churches relocate,
they require an organ transplant.

I always stay off the road on trash day.

Garbage collectors are rubbish drivers!

I started to write a salad pun,
but I tossed it.

I'm so good at sleeping,
I can do it with my eyes closed.

Odorless chemicals are
so confusing.
They make no scents!

What do prisoners use
to call each other?
Cell phones.

Will Livingston

Old skiers never die.

They just go downhill.

**Have you heard the pun
that's actually funny?**

If so, please tell it to me.

**Why do the best comedian chickens
lay useless eggs?**

Their yokes can't be beat!

Want to hear a pun about ghosts?

That's the spirit!

A lot of people hate clowns,
but I respect them.
Filling those big shoes is no small feat!

Why did the human cannonball
have to apply for unemployment?
The circus fired him!

A hen saw a doctor because she couldn't
get comfortable while trying to sleep.
He told her to lay off the eggs for a while

Why are hens great at fire drills?
They're used to egg-sitting.

Will Livingston

Every egg fears the end of the week.

That's fry day.

I used to wonder if there was a secret to making hard-boiled eggs taste good.

Then I cracked it.

A chicken coop has to have two doors.

If it had four, it would be a chicken sedan.

Why couldn't the chicken construction worker have children?

She only laid bricks.

Everyone knows you shouldn't have
too many cooks in a kitchen,
but the same is true of dish washers.
They get out of sink!

People using umbrellas always
seem to be under the weather.

I dissected an iris today.
It was an eye-opening experience.

Why did the aliens have a circus on
Saturn?
It has three rings!

Will Livingston

**My father was a stilt walker
before he died.**
I always looked up to him.

The circus lion ate the tightrope walker!
But at least it was a well-balanced meal.

I hate negative numbers so much...
I'll stop at nothing to avoid them!

**Did you know deer can jump
higher than the average house?**
*It's because of their strong hind legs.
Also, the average house can't jump.*

**Long fairy tales have
a tendency to dragon.**

**My friends say I'm addicted
to brake fluid.**

But I can stop at any time.

What did the grammarian owl say?

Whom whom.

**What do you call
a crocodile in a waistcoat?**

An investigator.

Will Livingston

You know what takes guts?

Making sausage.

What did one eye say to the other?

Between you and me, something smells.

What do you say to
a llama that loves picnicking?

Alpaca lunch.

Why didn't the photon
check any luggage at the airport?

It's travelling light.

**Did you hear about the glass blower
who accidentally inhaled?**

He got a sharp stomach pane.

**What do you call
a snail that isn't moving?**

An escar-stay.

**Did you hear about the new
corduroy pillowcases?**

They're really making headlines.

**Why couldn't the pony
sing in the choir?**

He was a little horse.

Will Livingston

I love my job making archery supplies.
Every workday has me
quivering with joy!

The past, the present, and the future
all walked into a bar...
It was tense.

I heard there's a dessert shortage,
but I think it's all a lack of pies.

Be kind to dentists.
They have fillings too, you know.

**Whoever stole the toilets from
the police station left no evidence.**

The cops have nothing to go on.

Why did the can crusher quit her job?

It was soda-pressing.

What do you call a broken can opener?

A can't opener.

**I was going to tell a joke
about a dead parrot...**

But it was way too macawbre.

Why do people love Switzerland?

Well, the flag is a big plus.

**Becoming vegetarian was
a huge missed steak.**

**How do trees feel
in the spring?**

Releaved.

**Why did the stumped detective
order Mexican food?**

He needed case ideas!

**Did you hear about
the sale on paddles?**

It was quite the oar-deal.

**Did you hear that
the devil is going bald?**

Yeah, there's gonna be hell toupee.

Why is Peter Pan always flying?

He Neverlands.

What language do bridges speak?

Span-ish.

Will Livingston

**Jokes about German sausage
are the wurst.**

Kids can't run in the campground!
They must ran, past tents.

I never use a straw.
They're for suckers.

**What do you call a lawyer
who can cook?**
A sue chef.

Plateaus are the highest form of flattery.

A sleepy driver got pulled over,

but refused to take a nap

when the officer told him to.

He resisted a rest!

Broken pencils are pointless.

Coffee has really bad luck.

It gets mugged every morning!

What do you call a dog

that thinks magic is real?

A labracadabrador believer.

This girl said she recognized me from the vegetarian club...

But I'd never met herbivore.

Never drink scotch while making whipped cream.

It's too whisky.

What do you call a dinosaur with an extensive vocabulary?

A thesaurus.

What does a triceratops sit on?

Its tricera-bottom.

I don't enjoy computer jokes.

Not one bit.

**Where should you keep a list
of all your favorite books?**

In a biblio-file.

I refuse to work with compost.

It's degrading.

**What do Russian kings order on their
pizzas?**

Czardines.

Will Livingston

Did you hear about the banker who left her job?

She just lost interest.

What happens when a piano falls down a mineshaft?

A-flat miner.

My friend fell into an upholstery machine.

He's fully recovered now.

How do you measure the quality of my puns?

A sighsmograph!

**You hear about the guy who turned
into a vampire <u>before</u> he was bitten?**

Premature edraculation is rough.

A termite walked into a bar and asked,

"Is the bar tender?"

**The local roofers union had
a big party last night.**

Today, they all have a terrible overhang.

**Why did the Spanish-speaking magician
vanish before the count of three?**

Because he disappeared without a tres!

Will Livingston

**Steak puns aren't common,
but when told just right...**
They're a rare medium well-done.

**If you fall behind on exorcist payments,
you might get repossessed.**

**Did you hear about the antiques
collector who found an old Coca-Cola
lamp?**
She was soda lighted.

**What do you give the pharaoh
who has everything?**
A gift cartouche.

If no two people see color the exact same way, then every hue is just...

A pigment of your imagination.

Did you hear about the guy who pickpocketed a toddler?

How could anybody stoop so low?!

My wife said my Boston cream pie was gritty, but I disagreed.

It was a rough custardy dispute.

My friend dove off a bridge in Paris.

He was okay, but also in Seine.

Will Livingston

**I heard putting snakes in your hair
can cure headaches.**

They say it's Medusa-nal.

What do you call a book on voyeurism?

A peeping tome.

I love foods cooked in oil.

I guess you could say I have refined taste.

**My local renaissance festival
is casting knights tomorrow at 4pm.**

Be there or be squire.

My friend David had his id stolen.

We just call him Dav now.

What do you call it when a cat wins first place at a dog show?

A cat-has-trophy!

A wealthy man once left his fortune to the San Andreas Nature Preserve.

He was generous to a fault.

Why are horses so cynical?

They're all neigh-sayers!

Will Livingston

Did you know that a single box of Borax can wash up to 15 dolphins?

It a great multi-porpoise cleaner.

Today I spent an hour watching two frogs croak at each other.

It was toadally ribbeting!

I started shrinking and my doctor said it'll take three weeks to cure!

I just have to be a little patient until then.

My dad's TV only plays in Spanish.

Poor SAP.

What did the conductor say

when she found her missing music?

Score!

How does Satan like his pasta?

Al Dante.

Why was the restless young man

a good swimmer?

The boy antsy.

Why did the mathematician

eat his prime rib whole?

He couldn't divide it!

Why do bulls make terrible salesmen?

They charge too much.

A man walked into a bar with a slab of asphalt under his arm and said,

"A beer please, and one for the road."

Where did the king keep his armies?

In his sleevies.

Did you hear about the cannibal social club?

Yeah, they really like to meat new people.

To the guy who invented zero:

Thanks for nothing!

Why did the golf club drink only water at the bar?

It was a designated driver.

I swatted a wasp today.

It was kind of a buzzkill.

I used a vending machine and it didn't give me my change.

I hate it when things don't make cents!

Will Livingston

Did you hear about the guy
who ate six cans of alphabet soup?
He had the biggest vowel movement ever.

Why did the young horse
practice galloping in private?
He didn't want to make a foal of himself.

I bought some shoes from
a drug dealer the other day.
I don't know what he laced them with,
but I've been tripping all day.

Singing quietly has never been my forte.

Did you hear about the overbooking fiasco at the introvert campout?

Everyone left because it was two in tents.

I dreamt a female horse trampled me in my sleep.

It was an awful night mare

I read about a prison that has started literature classes.

It has its prose and cons.

I was gonna tell a joke about sodium, but then I thought, "Na".

Will Livingston

**What did the pirate say
when he became an octogenarian?**
Aye matey!

**I bought my friend
an elephant for her room.**
*She thanked me, so I said,
"Don't mention it."*

What time do you go to the dentist?
Tooth hurty.

Geology rocks...
But geography is where it's at.

My optometrist's waiting room makes me nervous.

The other patients all look funny.

Did you hear about the secret pilot?

He spent much of his life in da skies.

My dog swallowed a bunch of Scrabble tiles last week.

His next trip outside spelled DISASTER

Why can't bikes stand unsupported?

They're two tired.

Will Livingston

**I turned invisible, so I tried
to make a doctor's appointment.**

Nobody could see me for weeks!

**Did you hear about the Norwegian robot
that analyzed a bird?**

It Scandinavian.

**Did you hear about the man who
swallowed several plastic horses?**

Docs described his condition as "stable"

I don't trust stairs.

They're always up to something.

**I think somebody added
more dirt to my vegetable garden.**
The plot thickens!

**Did you hear about the boat
that got crushed against its dock?**
Yet another casualty of pier pressure.

How do you find a Greek lunch?
Use a gyros-scope!

I just burned my Hawaiian pizza.
*I should've baked it
at aloha temperature!*

Will Livingston

**A bottle of omega-3 fell on
my head yesterday, but I'm okay.**
I only got super fish oil injuries.

I had problems with speed bumps...
But I'm slowly getting over them.

**Did you hear about the fork factory
with inconsistent quality control?**
*It was the best of tines,
it was the worst of tines.*

Why was Pavlov's hair so soft?
Classical conditioning.

**Did you hear about the explosion
at the cheese factory?**

De-brie went everywhere!

What kind of doctor is always on call?

An oncologist.

**What did the bartender say to the man
who walked in with jumper cables?**

"Don't start anything!"

The pacifist insect farmer got fired.

He wouldn't herd a fly.

Will Livingston

**My friend Marie left the navy
and changed her name to Mary.**
Why? "i before e, except after sea."

**My friend has fallen
head over heels for a new girl.**
She's a moonshiner, and he loves her still.

Why are noses in the middle of faces?
They like to be the scenter of attention.

Why did the pachyderm go to therapy?
*He felt irrelephant
to the people around him.*

"Shouldn't! Couldn't! Wouldn't!"

screamed the woman in the ER.

She was having contractions.

I've started investing in stocks:

beef, chicken, and vegetable.

Someday, I hope I'll be a bouillonaire.

Know what's getting popular?

Egg harvesting.

It's taking ova.

To be frank,

I'd have to change my name.

Will Livingston

**Did you hear about the
passionless baker?**
*He doesn't really care about his work,
he just kneads the dough.*

**Do you know that tadpoles
are natural storytellers?**
*Sadly, they lose their tales
when they grow up.*

**I wanted a magician at
my birthday party.**
My mom got a friendly clown instead.
It was disillusioning, but still a nice jester.

**Did you hear the police found
a misspelled message written in blood?**

They suspect it was a type-o.

**I just can't stop putting things in the
storage underneath my roof.**

I'm attic-ted.

**What do you call a small soda
<u>without</u> a tiny apple floating inside?**

Miniappleless Minisoda

I fired my masseuse today.

He just rubbed me the wrong way.

Will Livingston

Why are two helium isotopes so funny?
Hehe!

How do you make holy water?
You boil the hell out of it.

What do you call the lettuce left over after you make a salad?
The romainder!

Did you hear about the guy who could only hear high-pitched sounds?
He was in a world of treble.

**Why did the mermaid wear
a seashell bra?**

Because the d-shell bras were too big.

Why don't tennis players get married?

Because love means nothing to them.

**I got kicked out of an Indian restaurant
for asking too many questions.**

It's not my fault I'm naturally curry-ous!

**Afraid to admit you're in a pickle?
You can get it over with quickly...**

Just call it a dill-emma instead.

Will Livingston

How does Moses make coffee?

Hebrews it.

**If you're ever attacked by
a group of clowns...**

Go for the juggler.

**What do you call having
too many dogs?**

A roverdose.

I had amnesia once.

Maybe twice.

.

The saddest story I ever heard was about a man who dreamed of being an astronaut, but couldn't conquer his fear of the cramped spaceships.

Poor guy...he just needed space

What washes up on tiny beaches?

Microwaves.

A man's home is his castle.

In a manor of speaking.

If life gives you melons...

You might want to get tested for dyslexia.

Will Livingston

**What did the grape say
when it got stepped on?**
Nothing, but it let out a little wine.

What do you call a wine hangover?
The wrath of grapes.

Will glass coffins be a success?
Remains to be seen.

**I knew exactly what was going to
happen after my father died.**
His will was a dead giveaway.

Why don't kleptomaniacs like puns?

They always take things literally.

What's the difference

between a hippo and a Zippo?

One is really heavy,

The other is a little lighter.

Why do windmills like hard rock?

They're big metal fans.

Why did the performer break into song?

He couldn't find the key.

Will Livingston

Why are shotgun weddings so serious?

They're a matter of wife or death.

When a captain had to fire someone, why did he ask the ship barber to do it?

Because he was good at crewcuts.

I can't believe I got fired from the calendar factory.

All I did was take a day off.

A lot of money is tainted.

It taint yours and it taint mine.

What do you call a bee that can't make up its mind?

A maybe.

Every calendar's days...

Are numbered.

Hear about the new restaurant called karma?

There's no menu. You get what you deserve.

I went to a dozen stores yesterday trying to buy camouflage pants.

I couldn't find a single pair.

Will Livingston

When is alcohol always a solution?

When you're a chemist.

**How do you know
you're in too much debt?**

When you can't budge it.

**A police officer told me my dogs are
chasing people on bikes.**

That's ridiculous.

My dogs don't even own bikes.

I lost my mood ring today.

I don't know how I feel about that.

The furniture store keeps

calling me to come back.

All I wanted was one night stand.

I felt like everything

was coming my way.

Turns out I was in the wrong lane.

If you've seen one shopping center...

You've seen a mall.

I saw my first gray hair today.

I think I might dye.

Will Livingston

What did the janitor yell when he jumped out of the closet?

Supplies!

My grandfather had the heart of a lion.

And a lifetime ban from the zoo.

My father's last words were, "Be positive!"

We might have saved him if we'd only known his blood type.

What do you call the wife of a hippie?

A Mississippi.

What is the official job title of Santa's elves?

Subordinate clauses.

I didn't think I wanted a brain transplant.

Then the doctor changed my mind.

What country's capital has the fastest-growing population?

Ireland. It's Dublin every day.

In democracy, your vote counts.

In feudalism, your count votes.

Will Livingston

**There was a kidnapping
at school yesterday.**
Don't worry. He woke up.

**What do you call
a part-time band leader?**
A semiconductor.

Marathon runners with bad footwear
Suffer the agony of de feet.

**Did you hear about the man
who fell in the glass grinding machine?**
He made a spectacle of himself.

How does an attorney sleep?

First he lies on one side,

then he lies on the other.

A great round of acupuncture

Is a jab well done.

I tried to make a joke

about child labor...

But it was too immature to work.

I lost my job at the bank

on my very first day.

A woman asked me to check her balance,

so I pushed her over.

Will Livingston

I used to work in a blanket factory...
But it folded.

What are the strongest
days of the week?
Saturday and Sunday.
The rest are weekdays.

I hate funerals before noon.
I'm not really a mourning person.

If you have to quickly learn to fly,
is it still a crash course?

What was the fish doing in the tank?

Good question. It's not even a soldier!

**What's the difference between
a poorly dressed man on a bicycle and
a nicely dressed man on a tricycle?**

A tire.

**I feel much calmer since
I quit being a doctor.**

I got tired of always losing my patients.

Need an ark?

I Noah guy.

Will Livingston

**Protection should be used
on every conceivable occasion.**

I used to be indecisive…
But now I'm not so sure.

**A Freudian slip is when
you say one thing…**
But mean your mother.

What do you call the ghost of a chicken?
A poultry-geist.

Does the name Pavlov ring a bell?

I lost my job as a lumberjack.

I couldn't hack it, so they gave me the axe.

Dieting isn't so hard.

It's just mind over platter.

What is a gossip's favorite quality?

A great sense of rumor.

Why aren't dogs good dancers?

Because they have two left feet!

I thought about becoming a mime...

But I talked myself out of it.

Will Livingston

**My girlfriend thought I'd never be
able to make a car out of spaghetti...**
*You should've seen her face
when I drove pasta!*

**What did the duck say
when she purchased new lipstick?**
Put it on my bill!

**How do you organize
an outer space party?**
You planet.

My math teacher called me average.
How mean!

The "nature vs nurture" debate will go on forever, but one thing is certain:
If you choose an elevator
over an escalator,
that's a difference in upbringing.

My fortune cookie was empty.
How unfortunate!

Trigonometry is so confusing.
I wish I understood sine language.

Did you hear about the giraffe that escaped from the Atlanta zoo?
They found him in Savannah.

Will Livingston

**Reading while sunbathing
makes you well-red.**

I gave away dead batteries…
Free of charge!

**An invisible man
married an invisible woman.**
Their kids weren't much to look at.

**The mushroom is always
the life of the party.**
He's a real fungi.

No Pun Intended Volume Too

What did the coffee tell his date?

You're brew-tiful.

**What did the artery say
to the blood vessel?**

You're a little vein.

How do you fix a large horn?

With a tuba glue.

**Always C sharp before
crossing the road.**

Or else you might B flat!

Will Livingston

Did you know that mute frogs are immortal?

They can't croak!

Why was the coffee enthusiast always running late?

He was a chronic pro-caffeinator.

Why are peacocks so meticulous?

They show attention to de-tail.

When it comes to pizza jokes, it's all about the delivery.

Bladder infection?

Urine trouble.

**Vultures never check
their luggage.**

They prefer carrion.

**You shouldn't go into business
with a cheetah.**

They never prosper.

Don't lie to an x-ray tech.

They'll see right through you.

Will Livingston

**Orchestras should play more
than just classical music.**
They need to think outside the Bachs!

**Why did the balloons run away
from the concert?**
It was all pop music!

**Why are spiders great at
fixing networks?**
They always find bugs in the web.

**What do you get when you cross
a centipede with a parrot?**
A walkie-talkie.

**The big cat promised not to bite me,
but I think he was lion.**

Why did the appendix get dressed up?
*She heard a doctor is taking
her out tonight.*

**Did you hear that pidgeons
attacked a community theater?**
They cooed a stage!

Coffee and I make great partners.
*It keeps me awake,
I keep it grounded.*

Will Livingston

Why did the farmer buy a donkey?

He thought he might get a kick out of it.

Don't annoy a pediatrician.

They have little patients.

**It's raining cats and dogs out,
and you know what the worst part is?**

I stepped in a poodle.

Why did the marsupial get hired?

He was the most koala-fide.

Watch out for birds that sit on doorknobs.

They could fly off the handle at any moment!

How do you get ahold of a fish?

Just drop them a line.

I only ever remember 25 letters of the alphabet.

I can't recall why.

On the surface of things, whales are always blowing it.

Will Livingston

A cat ate some cheese and then waited for a mouse with baited breath.

Why did the chicken cross the playground?
To get to the other slide.

What happened when a skunk fell in the river?
He stank all the way to the bottom.

Why can't guitars relax?
Because they're so fretful.

My new girlfriend works at the zoo.

I think she's a keeper.

Giraffes aren't great comedians.

Their jokes always go over our heads.

**Are you sure this orchestra
is appropriate for children?**

I heard it has a lot of sax and violins.

**I was worried about
my transplant surgery...**

But the surgeon really de-livered.

Will Livingston

Beekeeping seems like a fun job...

As long as the insects beehive.

**My toddler threw his
cup of milk at me.**

How dairy!

**What's the difference between
deer nuts and beer nuts?**

Beer nuts are two dollars.

Deer nuts are under a buck.

I wrote a song about tortillas.

Actually, it's more of a rap.

I just burned 2,000 calories!
That's the last time I nap while
brownies are in the oven.

Never trust a crustacean.
They're all shellfish!

Watch out for horses, too.
They're frequently in stable.

People are often shocked when
they find that they hired
a terrible electrician.

Will Livingston

I'm reading a horror story in Braille,
and something bad is about to happen...
I can feel it!

I ordered a reversible jacket.
I can't wait to see how it turns out!

It's okay to watch an elephant bathe.
They always keep their trunks on.

Scientists have created
a flea from scratch.

What did one flag say to the other?
Nothing, it just waved.

I bought a boat because it was for sail.

Why do lawyers always dress so nice?
They love a good lawsuit.

I made ten submissions to a pun contest, hoping at least one would win. Unfortunately . . .
NO PUN IN TEN DID.

AFTER WORDS

Thenceforward

Subsequently

Ensuing

Next

Etc

!

Made in the USA
Middletown, DE
16 October 2023

40825657R00076